SOLOS FOR THE SANCTUARY
GOSPEL
8 PIANO SOLOS FOR THE CHURCH PIANIST

Arranged by Glenda Austin

ISBN 978-1-4803-5251-3

WILLIS MUSIC

EXCLUSIVELY DISTRIBUTED BY

HAL•LEONARD®
CORPORATION
7777 W. BLUEMOUND RD. P.O. BOX 13819 MILWAUKEE, WI 53213

© 2014 by The Willis Music Co.
International Copyright Secured   All Rights Reserved

Visit Hal Leonard Online at
www.halleonard.com

PREFACE

This compilation contains some of my very favorite "pop" songs of the church. Age-wise, they are in a gray area: despite being around forever—and most likely they will be around for many years—they are not quite public domain. Here are a couple of suggestions for playing them. First and foremost, please feel free to interpret and incorporate them in a way that fits your mood, style and ability. Simply stated: *Don't hesitate to be creative.* I included some bare-bones editing such as tempo suggestions and dynamic markings—if I attempted to edit phrasing and place a *rubato* in every measure of every piece, it would be too much! In other words, I am granting you, the performer, a special artistic license to express yourself in your own unique and individual way.

Now for a bit of trivia about some of my selections. My sister Gloria Sanborn and I have played piano and organ duets for more than 30 years. Both medleys—"The King Is Coming" and "How Excellent Is Thy Name"—have special meaning because we still play them annually. In all honesty, I enjoy playing them now as much as ever. And just a couple of weeks before writing this note, I performed the first arrangement in this book: "How Great Thou Art." Of course, that's a universal favorite, no matter what your denomination! The second selection, "My Tribute" by Andraé Crouch, is not seasonal but the lyrics definitely convey a message of gratitude. I often play it as an offertory before Thanksgiving. Honestly, every piece in this book evokes a special and personal memory. Suffice it to say, I love them all, and with pleasure my arrangements are now yours.

It is my wish that this book will provide you another opportunity to "make a joyful noise unto the Lord." May God bless you as you use your talent to serve Him.

All the best,

Glenda Austin

CONTENTS

How Great Thou Art

for Charmaine Siagian

Words by Stuart K. Hine
Traditional Swedish Folk Tune Adapted by Stuart K. Hine
Arranged by Glenda Austin

My Tribute

for Judith Shaw

Words and Music by
Andraé Crouch
Arranged by Glenda Austin

Sweet, Sweet Spirit

for Lois Nassen

Words and Music by
Doris Akers
Arranged by Glenda Austin

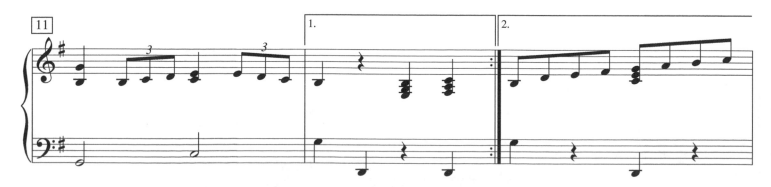

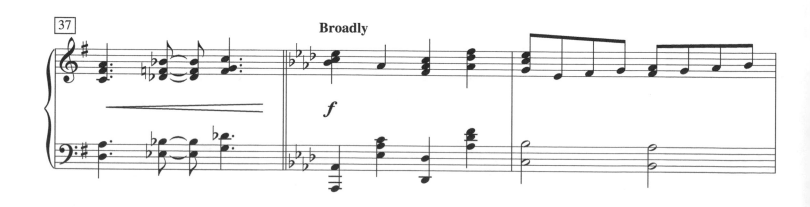

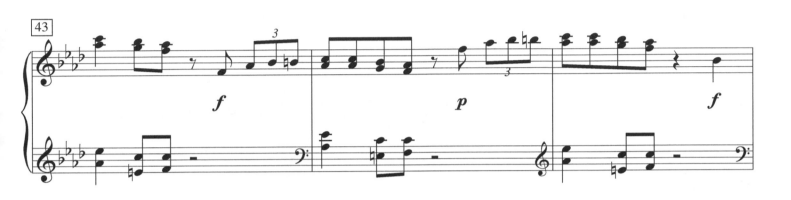

Soon and Very Soon

for Sandra Siler

Words and Music by
Andraé Crouch
Arranged by Glenda Austin

Mansion Over the Hilltop

for Bethany Mullins

Words and Music by
Ira F. Stanphill
Arranged by Glenda Austin

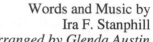

Victory in Jesus

for Carolyn Orbin

Words and Music by
E.M. Bartlett
Arranged by Glenda Austin

The King Is Coming/
We Shall Behold Him

for Sherry Frush

Words by William J. and Gloria Gaither
and Charles Millhuff
Music by William J. Gaither
Arranged by Glenda Austin

Expressively, not hurried

mf

With pedal

WE SHALL BEHOLD HIM

Words and Music by Dottie Rambo

Più mosso

(THE KING IS COMING)
Triumphantly, slower

How Excellent Is Thy Name

with **Christ Arose / I've Just Seen Jesus / Because He Lives**

for Marcus Van Dorn

Arranged by Glenda Austin

HOW EXCELLENT IS THY NAME
Words and Music by Dick Tunney, Melodie Tunney and Paul Smith

Energetically! ♩ = c. 144

With pedal

dim. poco a poco

CHRIST AROSE (Low In the Grave He Lay)
Words and Music by Robert Lowry

mp

I'VE JUST SEEN JESUS
Words by Gloria Gaither
Music by William J. Gaither and Danny Daniels

BECAUSE HE LIVES
Words by William J. and Gloria Gaither
Music by William J. Gaither

SOLOS FOR THE SANCTUARY
by Glenda Austin

Exciting piano solos for church pianists everywhere!
These excellent arrangements by Glenda Austin may be used for
church and recital performances, or simply for personal enjoyment.

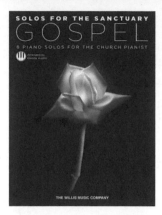

SOLOS FOR THE SANCTUARY – GOSPEL

8 Piano Solos
for the Church Pianist

How Excellent Is Thy Name/I've Just Seen Jesus/Because He Lives (Medley) • How Great Thou Art • The King Is Coming/We Shall Behold Him (Medley) • My Tribute • Mansion Over the Hilltop • Soon and Very Soon • Sweet, Sweet Spirit • Victory in Jesus.

00121443 ....$10.99

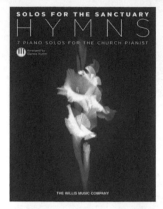

SOLOS FOR THE SANCTUARY – HYMNS

7 Piano Solos
for the Church Pianist

Amazing Grace • Be Thou My Vision • It Is Well With My Soul • Jesus Loves Me/He Keeps Me Singing (*medley*) • My Jesus, I Love Thee • Shall We Gather at the River?/On Jordan's Stormy Banks (*medley*) • What a Friend We Have in Jesus.

00416901 ....$9.99

SOLOS FOR THE SANCTUARY – WORSHIP

9 Piano Solos
for the Church Pianist

Above All • Change My Heart Oh God • Give Thanks • Great Is the Lord • How Great Is Our God • How Majestic is Your Name • In Christ Alone • There Is a Redeemer • You Are My All in All.

00101918................................$10.99

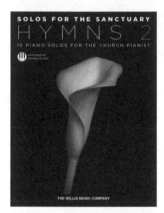

SOLOS FOR THE SANCTUARY – HYMNS 2

10 Piano Solos
for the Church Pianist

Blessed Assurance • Great Is Thy Faithfulness • Holy, Holy, Holy • Jesus Paid It All • Just As I Am • Nothing But the Blood • Praise the Lord! Ye Heavens Adore Him! • To God Be the Glory • Trust and Obey • Turn Your Eyes Upon Jesus/Softly and Tenderly (*medley*).

00295567 ....$10.99

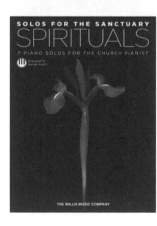

SOLOS FOR THE SANCTUARY – SPIRITUALS

7 Piano Solos
for the Church Pianist

The Gospel Train • Joshua (Fit the Battle of Jericho) • My Lord, What a Morning • Rock-a-My Soul • Swing Low, Sweet Chariot • There Is a Balm in Gilead • Wayfaring Stranger.

00416897................................$8.99

SOLOS FOR THE SANCTUARY – CHRISTMAS

8 Piano Solos
for the Church Pianist

Angels We Have Heard on High • Bring a Torch, Jeannette, Isabella • The First Noel • Go, Tell It on the Mountain • God Rest Ye Merry, Gentlemen • He Is Born • Sing We Now of Christmas • What Child Is This?

00416488................................$8.99

WILLIS MUSIC

EXCLUSIVELY DISTRIBUTED BY

HAL•LEONARD®

willispianomusic.com

f **facebook.com/willispianomusic**

 willispiano